# FORTUNE

## TELLING

# FORTUNE
## TELLING

LORENZ BOOKS

This edition published in 1998 by Lorenz Books
an imprint of Anness Publishing Limited
Hermes House, 88-89 Blackfriars Road, London SE1 8HA

© Anness Publishing Limited 1992, 1998

This edition published in the USA by Lorenz Books
Anness Publishing Inc., 27 West 20th Street, New York, NY 10011;
(800) 354-9657

This edition distributed in Canada by Raincoast Books
8680 Cambie Street, Vancouver, British Columbia V6P 6M9

ISBN 1-85967-766-5

A CIP catalogue record for this book is available from the British Library

Publisher: JOANNA LORENZ
Creative Director: PETER BRIDGEWATER
Text: DAVID V. BARRETT
Original Illustrations: IVAN HISSEY

Printed and bound in Singapore
1 3 5 7 9 10 8 6 4 2

The Publishers would like to thank all those who kindly
gave permission to reproduce visual material in this book;
every effort was made to identify copyright holders and
we apologise for any inadvertent omissions.

# CONTENTS

# PREFACE

There are occasions after a **DINNER PARTY** when the company is not **serious-minded** enough to play Bridge, nor light-minded enough to play party games. A brief recital by one of the number at the pianoforte may be a pleasurable after-dinner interlude, but we have all spent too many evenings hearing Viennese waltzes poorly played, or suffering the cracked and tuneless voice of one guest when all are singing uplifting songs *ensemble*.

Few are the guests who, as a change from these usual diversions, would raise objections to their fortunes being told. Moreover, this is suitable for old and young, and especially suitable for mixed company. It is an excellent diversion on *BOXING DAY*, when one's guests will have eaten and drunk their fill that day and the previous, and are **desirous** of unusual entertainment.

At most dinner parties there will be one, most probably a maiden lady of mature years, who can *Read the Cards*, or if the hostess's maid or cook be brought above stairs she may be persuaded to *Read the Tea-Leaves* for the company assembled, though as her sensibilities and proprieties will not be those expected in a Drawing Room she should be warned severely beforehand to 🖝

watch her tongue lest she offend any of the guests by any **injudicious interpretations.**

My very good and old friend the *Rev. Dr. Armytage Ware M.A.,* knowing of my intention to write this little book, has requested that I warn against dabbling with the spirit world, through the consulting of mediums, table-tapping, the use of *OUI-JA BOARDS* and so forth. With this I concur, and declare that within these few pages one may find many hours of innocent amusement, such as is fitting in all companies, and such as would give offence to none, including to my esteemed and venerable friend.

In this same spirit, then, I commend this little work to you.

D. VICKERS BARRETT, ST STEPHEN'S DAY 1900

# READING THE PALM

◆◆◆

IT IS TO BE marvelled at the secrets to be revealed in that most familiar object, the **PALM** of one's **HAND**. The course of one's entire life may be found in the *Lines* written therein: one's vocation and success, intellectual and artistic PROPENSI-TIES, *romantic inclinations* and family life, even one's child-hood ailments and future health, are all here for the initiated to see.

Although the lamps may be dimmed in the remainder of the Drawing Room, it is of the highest importance that there be a good light for the Reader to see the Palm of her "Client's" Hand clearly. We say "her", for the practice of Chiromancy or Chirognomy is by custom performed by the *fairer sex*, who are more attuned, perhaps by the *intuition* often ascribed to them, to the revelation of the secrets of the HAND.

The Reader (especially if she be the *cook* who, if she had a country upbringing, may already be well-skilled in PALM-READING) should be warned previously not to *reveal* anything of **Dark Import**, such as would spoil the enjoyment of the evening.

For a full Reading, both Hands should be examined, for the Left Hand is said to hold the most inner secrets of the self, while the Right reveals how its owner fares in the world. (If the Client be *sinistral*, or "left-handed", he should tell the Reader, as the meanings of the two Hands are then reversed.)

# TYPES *of* HAND

*A*ccording to the Frenchman Casimir d'Arpentigny, and the famous Palmist Cheiro, there are *Seven Types* of Hand.

☞ The **ELEMENTARY HAND** is large and thick, with few Lines, and short broad Fingers. It is typical of the Labouring Classes; its owner may have little imagination, but he will be a strong worker.

☞ The **SQUARE (or PRACTI-CAL) HAND** is square in shape, with the Fingers all of about the same length. These people span all classes; they are practical, methodical, honest, and orthodox in their beliefs.

☞ The **SPATULATE (or ACTIVE) HAND** looks like a spatula or *spade;* its Finger-tips similarly are wider at the tips than is usual. Its owner is active, energetic, ambitious and independent.

☛ The **PHILOSOPHIC (or KNOTTY) HAND** is bony and angular, with thin Fingers and knotty knuckles. These people are intelligent and imaginative, and make good Scholars.

☛ The **CONIC (or ARTISTIC) HAND** is of medium size, with a tapered Palm and likewise tapered, pointed Fingers. Its owner may be artistic, certainly sensitive to art and music, and Emotional.

☛ The beautiful **PSYCHIC (or IDEALISTIC) HAND** has a narrow Palm with long, slender Fingers. Its owner is equally delicate, trusting and compassionate, sensitive and idealistic.

☛ The **MIXED HAND** has elements of any two or more of these six, and denotes a mixture of the relevant qualities. Whichever they are, this person will be versatile and changeable.

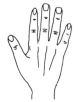

# THE MOUNTS

◆◆◆

*T*he *padded swellings* on the Palm are known as the *Mounts;* they should be well-rounded and firm, neither flat nor puffy. For most of us some of them are over-developed or under-developed, revealing an excess or a lack of the relevant Quality.

The *Mount of Venus* is the well-padded part of the Palm at the base of the Thumb. This shows love and devotion; the cook (if it be she performing the Reading) should be requested not to refer to the *sensual* nature of a well-padded Mount of Venus.

The *Mount of the Moon,* which lies opposite, on the percussive edge of the Palm, shows imagination and creativity.

The *Mount of Jupiter,* at the base of the Index Finger, signifies power, good fortune and leadership.

The *Mount of Saturn,* below the Middle Finger, shows a prudent, thoughtful, well-balanced person.

The *Mount of Apollo,* below the Ring Finger, signifies æsthetic appreciation, and a pleasing personality.

The *Mount of Mercury,* below the Little Finger, shows liveliness, wit and verbal dexterity.

Across the middle of the Palm, on the Thumb side, the *Mount of Mars Active* denotes strength and great physical courage.

Opposite, on the percussive side, the *Mount of Mars Passive* denotes quiet courage, and moral virtue.

In the hollow of the Palm the *Plain of Mars,* if it is Well-Developed, shows capability and practicality.

INDEPENDENCE
OF THOUGHT

MENTAL

FIRST
KNOT

FIRST
PHALANX

SECOND
PHALANX

INDEPENDENCE OF ACTION

INDEPENDENCE OF WILL

LOGIC
OR REASON

THIRD
PHALANX

B

MOUNT
LUNA

PERCU

⟨13⟩

*The supple-jointed thumb*    *The firm-iointed thumb*

*The clubbed thumb*    *The waist-like thumb*    *The straight thumb*    *The elementary thumb*

*The square with smooth joints*    *The pointed*    *The knotty*

# THE FINGERS
## *and the* THUMB

---

*E*ach FINGER represents the characteristics of one of the ancient *Greek Gods* with which we are all familiar. Examine its length in comparison to the other Fingers, and study most carefully the proportionate length of each *phalanx* or joint of the Finger. The first *phalanx* (that which contains the Finger-nail) denotes mental characteristics and intuition; the middle practical, financial and business; while the third indicates the material and earthy qualities of the Sensations, such as ought not to be revealed if they might cause embarrassment to any there present.

The length of each *phalanx* and each Finger overall shows the strength of each Quality represented therein.

The *Index Finger*, called JUPITER after the King of the Gods, shows strength of character; the man who is a born leader of men.

The *Middle Finger*, called SATURN, shows a serious, deep-thinking person, such as would do well in the Sciences.

The *Ring Finger*, called APOLLO after the Greek Sun God, shows the degree to which one is emotionally stable; it also reveals talents in the Arts.

The *Little Finger*, called MERCURY after the Messenger of the Gods, shows a powerful intellect and a skill with words.

The *Thumb*, standing out on its own, is the strongest of all the digits, and may sometimes remedy such faults or deficiencies as might be revealed by the other Fingers. The first *phalanx* represents will-power, and the second the reasoning powers; there is no third, except it be the *Mount of Venus*, which shows as we have seen such qualities as are not seemly to be possessed in excess, though in moderation this Mount displays those virtues to be desired in a Devoted Wife and Mother.

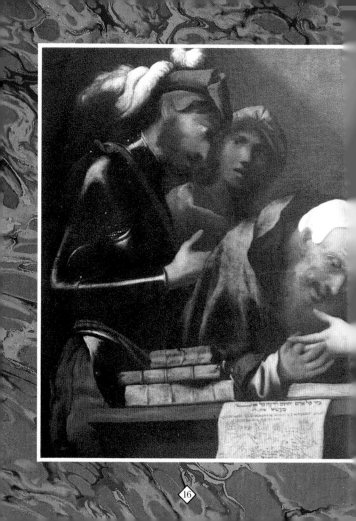

# THE LINES
## *of the* PALM

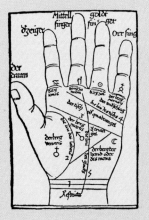

*Only now do we come to those* LINES *which the
ignorant think are the whole matter of* **PALM-
READING**. *Not every person has every Line,
and the absence of a particular Line should
cause no distress; indeed, it would seem to show
that the owner of the Hand has no particular
need to worry himself about matters pertaining
to that Line.*

This should also be conso-
lation to those who are possessed of a peculiarly short **LIFE
LINE**, or one which is broken;
the foolish and credulous believe that such a person will
die young, even though all the
weight of Empirical Evidence
shows this belief to be not only

a folly but the very essence of that blatant men-
dacity so often expressed by the ignorant and
malicious. Pay no heed to them.

If you desire to know when events foretold in
the Lines will occur, remember that one-twelfth
of an inch is supposed to show the passage of
about two years; but such measurement is notori-
ously difficult, and should not be attempted
except by one with **CONSIDERABLE EXPERI-
ENCE** of Palm-Reading.

The LIFE LINE is the
easiest to find: it curves
around the MOUNT OF
VENUS, springing from be-
tween the base of the Index
Finger and the inside of the
base of the Thumb. If the
curve is wide, it portrays an
open, generous person of
Warm and Gregarious
Nature; if narrow, one who is more private
and inward-looking.

The Life Line shows, instead of the **LENGTH** of life, rather its quality, its strength and intensity. **LACUNÆ** in the Line may show problems pertaining to health, or may reveal major changes to come in the owner's life. A Line of both good length and depth denotes rude health throughout one's life.

The **HEART LINE** is the higher of the two broadly horizontal Lines, and curves from near the base of the Index Finger to the percussive edge of the Hand. This Line shows emotional characteris-tics, in particular those per-taining to affairs of the Heart. Ideally it possesses no breaks or cross-bars, neither does it fade, and if it be situated as described, the person with this Line is warm, caring and de-pendable: the ideal partner for life. If the line is straight, ☛

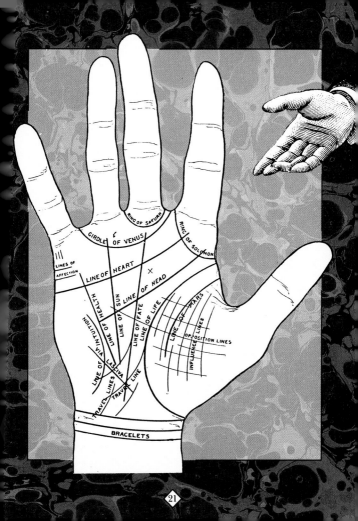

then the heart is ruled by the head; if it is weak or faded then the person is insecure in their emotions. Do not trust your heart to one whose Heart Line possesses little chains, for they will be fickle with their affections. Breaks in the line show a **BROKEN HEART**; but be comforted, for the Line will recommence before too long!

The HEAD LINE is the lower of the two horizontal lines and begins close to, and is often conjoined with, the **LIFE LINE**. This Line gives a clear picture of the strength of the person's mind and will. If it should lie straight, then its owner will be possessed of a fine, logical, analytical mind; if it curves down towards the **MOUNT OF LUNA** then the mental faculties will be more intuitive and imaginative.

If its beginning is within the Life Line this shows no harm, unless the separation of the two be much delayed, which denotes the late development of its owner. If it begins well above the Life Line, the person will be strongly independent, perhaps even Reckless; but if below, they will habitually display nervousness.

**BEWARE** of the person whose Heart and Head Lines are one, a deep and angry slashing across the Palm, for this person will be extreme in his beliefs, his emotions and his behaviour. Whatever he approaches it will be with unreasoning single-minded devotion and intensity, and he will brook no argument or opposition.

The FATE LINE should start at or near the wrist and pass more-or-less vertically through the hollow of the Palm (the **PLAIN OF MARS**) to end near the base of the Middle (**SATURN**) Finger. A well-formed Line shows responsibility and success in one's career; a gentleman with this Line will be a good provider for his family. If the Line starts at the wrist it shows self-reliance; if from the Life Line, it betokens strong family influences, perhaps a career in the family business. If starting from the **MOUNT OF LUNA**, it shows a changeable career with much uncertainty, perhaps in the ARTS. If it begins high up the Hand it shows a late start and much hard labour needed to bring success in one's career.

The APOLLO LINE is called by some the
Sun, Success, Fortune or Fame Line. Usually a
short vertical line running parallel to the Fate
Line, but closer to the percussive edge of the
Hand, and ideally to the base of the Ring
(APOLLO) Finger, this Line reveals UNUSUAL
SUCCESS, beyond that which might reasonably
be expected through normal hard work. If this
is to occur, it will usually be in the "mature"
years of life, when one is the Master of one's
abilities and Talents. Rare indeed is an Apollo
Line beginning low in the Hand, showing the
recognition and fame enjoyed by a musical
prodigy, perhaps, or a young and gifted actress.

# Hamley Bros Ltd

## Fortune - Telling Cup and Saucer

This Cup makes tea-leaf fortune-telling possible to everyone, and is the cause of much fun and amusement.

Price, complete with book of instructions 5/6, post free 6/6

## The "Rameses" Fortune-Telling Cards

These Cards are highly finished with gilt edges. Full instructions given with each pack.

Price 3/6,    post free 3/10

## Hamley's Cabinet
### of
## Jokes and Catches

Containing a fine assortment of the latest practical jokes. Endless fun may be had out of one of these.

Prices    1/- and 2/6
Post free    1/3 and 2/10

## Crystal-Gazing Balls

| Sizes | 1 in. | 2 in. |
|---|---|---|
| Price | 9/6 | 11/6 |

Very Superior, in Case
Price   15/6 and 42/-

### CHEAPER QUALITY BALLS
Sizes

| 1 in. | 2 in. | 2½ in. | 3 in. | 4 in. |
|---|---|---|---|---|
| | | Price | | |
| 4/6 | 6/6 | 8/6 | 11/9 | 16/6 |

Packing 9d. extra.

## Trouble Wit

This consists of a specially prepared paper from which several shapes can be formed with very little practice.

Price 2/-. Larger size 2/6

### Rainbow Coloured
Trouble Wits, price 4/-
Professional size    7/6
(postage extra).

# READING
# THE CARDS

I<small>F THERE</small> be a local Gypsy-woman perhaps known to your servants, it might provide a pleasurable *diversion* for your guests if she Read the Cards after a dinner party. Although our more Liberal clergy, who work so devotedly (and with so little reward or thanks) amongst the poor, tell us that the Gypsy-folk (or as they prefer, the *Romanies*) are not the Thieves and Rogues we have been led to believe, nevertheless the servants should be warned to watch her at all times, if she eat with them before being brought upstairs. ☞

You should agree beforehand whether she be paid all at once (in which case a shilling will be sufficient payment for an hour or two's entertainment), or whether each "Client" should "cross her palm with silver" separately and individually. Your dinner-guests must also be told which arrangement has been agreed, to avoid embarrassment.

However, the skill of READING THE CARDS is not a difficult one for the hostess herself to master, though at first sight there seem a lot to learn.

There are at least as many ways of READING THE CARDS as there are Cards in the Pack. Some are very complicated and take a long time to perform, both in their layout and in their interpretation. As we imagine that you would wish to have some several Readings during the course of the evening (though all authorities agree that you should never perform a Reading for the same person more than once in twenty-four hours), we will only give two of the simplest methods here.

Each method is with the re-duced (or *Italian*) pack of only thirty-two cards, without us-ing the "pip" cards from 2 to 6, though there are also many methods using the full English pack of fifty-two cards. With the normal "double-ended" cards it is necessary to mark with a pencil one end to be "top", so that "reversed" mean-ings may also be drawn from the Cards.

## A GYPSY METHOD

*In a traditional Gypsy method, here simplified, one first selects a card to be the Significator for the "Client" or "Querent", according to the following table.*

*Ladies*
Fair-haired & mature: Queen of Diamonds
Fair-haired & young: Queen of Hearts
Dark-haired & mature: Queen of Spades
Dark-haired & young: Queen of Clubs

*Gentlemen*
Fair-haired & mature: King of Diamonds
Fair-haired & young: King of Hearts
Dark-haired & mature: King of Spades
Dark-haired & young: King of Clubs

*"Fair-haired" should also be taken to include grey, while the usual dividing-line between "young" and "mature" is the age of forty, though some discretion should be employed here with the ladies!* 🐦

The Querent shuffles the thirty-two cards
thoroughly and cuts them (with the left hand)
by placing them in three piles, reversing the
centre pile, and placing the right-hand pile on
top of the centre, and these two together on top
of the left-hand pile. The cards are shuffled
again, and the top and bottom cards removed
for later use. The remaining thirty cards are
then dealt in three rows of ten.

The top row shows Significant People and
Events in the Querent's **PAST**, the middle row
the **PRESENT**, and the bottom row the
**FUTURE**; the three rows should be interpreted
in this order, taking especial note of the prepon-
derance of any suit, or any groups of cards
which seem significant. The Court cards, of
course, represent people, as in the list below,
while the "pip" cards represent emotions, events
or circumstances. The skill of the Reader is to
draw each row of ten cards together into a co-
herent **STORY**, rather than simply detailing the
individual cards. The positioning of the Significator shows which row – Past, Present or
Future – is of the highest importance, as the
Querent is most intimately involved in that
row's "story".

The two cards earlier laid aside may now be
brought out as a "Surprise", which may be disturbing or beneficial.

# THE
# TEMPLE of FORTUNE

◆◆◆

          This spread was devised by an *18th-century* Paris wigmaker called Alliette, who achieved fame as "Etteilla" for his study of Tarot cards.

    The cards are well-shuffled and cut as before, and then dealt out as in the diagram: the two pillars of the outer arch first (each containing six cards, the right, then the left, laid *from bottom to top*), then the entire inner arch, with four cards *up* the right-hand pillar, five across the top *to the left*, and four more *down* the left-hand pillar; finally, the remaining seven cards are laid across the top *from left to right*.

    The *outer arch* (the exterior walls of the temple) shows the major events and influences of the *past* (the right-hand pillar of six), the *present* (the seven cards along the top) and the *future* (the left-hand pillar), in each case reading the cards in the order in which they were laid down.

    The *inner arch* shows minor or modifying influences: the four cards in the inner right-hand pillar applying to the Reading already given for the *past*, the five along the top to the *present*, and the four in the left-hand pillar to the *future*.

## THE MEANINGS OF THE CARDS

"DARK" and "FAIR" can refer not only to the colour of hair, but also to the eyes, the complexion generally, and sometimes to the *nature*.

If a card is reversed, it generally has a "negative" or un-pleasant meaning, usually the reverse of the "positive" meaning given here.

**HEARTS** concern emotions and matters of the heart

*Ace:* Happiness in the home
*King:* A fair and fair-minded, generous man, probably professional
*Queen:* A fair, affectionate and Attractive woman
*Knave:* A happy and faithful young friend
*10:* Good fortune, success, happiness, triumph over difficulties
*9:* A happy result, a fulfilled wish, Good Luck
*8:* Friendship, romance, marriage
*7:* Domestic harmony, settled love

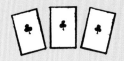

**CLUBS** concern power, ability, business matters

*Ace:* Success in business, prosperity
*King:* A dark man, helpful, reliable, faithful
*Queen:* A dark woman, highly romantic, perhaps wealthy
*Knave:* A good, dependable, reliable friend
*10:* Money, great prosperity, perhaps with a Dark Side
*9:* Unexpected financial gain; a wealthy marriage
*8:* Dark young lady or youth; small amount of money
*7:* Dark child; small but troublesome financial matters ☞

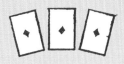

**DIAMONDS** concern business, finance and travel

*Ace:* An important letter, document, message or (marriage) proposal

*King:* A fair man with power, authority: perhaps official or military

*Queen:* A dangerously attractive fair woman, frivolous or malicious

*Knave:* A messenger, a minor official, probably Untrustworthy

*10:* Success with a change, of home or job, or a journey

*9:* A surprise gift, new business deal, but may lose friends

*8:* Pleasant journey in country, picnic, party, small gift

*7:* A present, invitation, surprising news

**SPADES** concern Fate, misfortune, troubles, disagreements, deep loss

*Ace:* Pleasure in love, but legal problems (Reversed: sorrow, death)

*King:* Dark man, successful, ambitious, dangerous, perhaps a lawyer

*Queen:* Dark (probably) widow or divorcée, cunning and unscrupulous

*Knave:* Dark, young, ill-mannered, treacherous person

*10:* Bad luck, worrying letter, jealousy, unhappiness

*9:* Illness, failure, misfortune, conflict, defeat

*8:* Possibly avoidable threats to enterprises; Avoid Risks

*7:* Worry, burdens

# THE TAROT CARDS

In recent years there have come to these shores those brightly coloured and strangely designed cards known as TAROT or, as the Italians call them, *Tarocchi*. In France it is a popular practice to play a game with these cards, of the nature of bridge or whist, but those who use the Tarot cards in this country also claim for them quite marvellous *predictive powers*.

The cards are divided into two groups: the *Major*, which consists of twenty-two beautiful pictures of such people as High Priests and Emperors, and their female equivalents, and of such virtues as Temperance and Justice, and of the Sun and Moon and Star; and the *Minor* which, as with ordinary playing cards, consists of four suits, though they be of different names, being *CUPS, STAVES, COINS* or *DENIERS*, and *SWORDS* instead of the familiar *Hearts, Clubs, Diamonds* and *Spades*, and they have also one extra Court card, the Knight.

There are thus seventy-eight of these cards altogether, and each has a different divinatory meaning, the which makes their Reading a Complex and Skilled Matter which we are not competent to expound, nor is there, truly, space in this small book for such an exposition.

Only shall it be said, then, that these cards are very Ancient in their origin, coming, so the Egyptologists tell us, from that land of mystery; and that they are said to contain many hidden *truths;* and that some, such as my learned clerical friend the Rev. Dr. Armytage Ware, have been known to decry them as "The Devil's Picture-Book", for they contain amongst their number one card showing in gruesome detail the Devil, and another morbidly illustrating Death, and yet one more depicting a Hanged Man.

These are, we suggest, but three of seventy-eight cards, and the beauty and mystery of the Tarot cards, and their astonishing power when interpreted by a skilled practitioner, make their Reading by such a person something to be much desired; in addition to which, because of their relative rarity, such a Reading at one's *dinner party* would surely set that occasion apart from the other social events in one's circle.

The Emperor | The Pope | The Lovers | The Fool

Wheel of Fortune | Strength | The Hanged Man | The Tower

The Star | The Moon | The Juggler | The High Priestess

**III**

L'IMPERATRICE

*The Empress*

**VII**

LE CHARIOT

*The Chariot*

**VIII**

LA JUSTICE

*Justice*

**VIIII**

L'ERMITE

*The Hermit*

**XIII**

LA MORT

*Death*

**XIIII**

TEMPERANCE

*Temperance*

**XV**

LE DIABLE.

*The Devil*

**XVIIII**

LE SOLEIL

*The Sun*

**XX**

LE JUGEMENT

*Judgement*

**XXI**

LE MONDE

*The World*

ROI DE DENIER

*The King of Coins*

VALET DES ÉPÉES

*The Prince of Swords*

# READING THE TEA-LEAVES

WE ARE ASSURED that it will be necessary to recruit neither the *maid* nor the *cook* for this ever-popular amusement, as in every company assembled, in our experience, where there be a half-dozen or more ladies present, and more especially if some amongst these be of more mature years, there will be at least one who is proficient in READING THE TEA-LEAVES, or *Tasseography* as the experts call it.

The preliminaries to READING THE TEA-LEAVES are simplicity itself, and are familiar, if not absolutely second nature, to every lady of more than early childhood years and also, in these more advanced days, to not a few gentlemen also.

The tea is made in the usual way, for it is essential to the Reading that it be drunk by the Client before its residue may be examined. It must be poured into the cup without the use of a strainer, for a strainer would remove that very residue of leaves which we desire to study! If it is possible, the simplest white china or porcelain cups should be employed for the purpose as, however beautiful a contribution to the home the finest patterned tea-service may make, the designs are sadly obscurative of the more subtle patterns of leaves. A wide-bowled cup is also to be preferred, as providing a *greater expanse* upon which to READ THE LEAVES.

Finally, although any type of tea may be employed, it has been found that China tea provides clearer pictures than Indian, for the latter may sometimes be "dusty",

and give only confused and muddy pictures. In contra-distinction those created by the leaves of China tea are always clear and informative, for the Oriental Chinee is rightly known for his fabled powers of divination.

Once the tea has been consumed, with care not to drink the leaves, a little of the amber liquid should be left in the bottom of the cup. The Client should "swirl" this drop around the cup three times in a clockwise direction, holding the cup by her left hand, then up-end the vessel onto its saucer to allow the ☞

liquid to drain away. She should count slowly to seven before setting the cup to rights again, turning the handle to face the Reader.

The handle represents the Client, and her home, and the present-day. Patterns to the left of the handle show events in her past, and those to the right events in her future, the distance from the handle being proportionate to the time involved. These *relative* positions also portray physical distance and direction of travel, so that some will appear to be moving *towards* the handle, while others move *away*. A measure of TIME is also to be found in the *depth* of the cup, in that patterns near to the *rim* or drinking edge portray events occurring in the Present time, while those in the depths of the bowl foreshadow those of the Future.

It is said by some that a sign appearing in the very bottom of the cup portends misfortune.

The patterns caused by the leaves and fragments of stalk of the Tea-plant are not easy to recognise for one new to the practice; it will be found to be necessary to employ all of one's faculties of imagination and intuition, of which those of the *fairer sex* are well-endowed, to discover meaningful shapes amongst them.

## THE SYMBOLS *in the* TEA-CUP

*Signs of Good Luck include* RINGS, *which show an approaching marriage, unless the Ring be at the very bottom of the cup, in which case the unhappy pair will become separated;* TRI-ANGLES, *if they be pointing upwards, for the opposite is misfortune;* CLOVERS, *which show the Holy Trinity, unless they be four-leaved, which are a sign of especial Good Fortune;* HORSE-SHOES, *which since ancient times have been a sign of Good Fortune; most* FLOWERS, TREES *and* ANIMALS, *for they are of God's Nature;* CROWNS, *for they show authority, trust, honour and respect, and re-mind us of Her Glorious Majesty Victoria in the seventh decade of her Reign; and the number "7", which is God's own number and so can only be good.*

*We shall now set forward some of the signs and symbols most frequently to be observed in the* TEA-CUP.

# A–Z

*Acorn:* success in money
*Anchor:* success and prosperity from a voyage
*Angel:* good news
*Apple:* achievement, a desire for Knowledge
*Arch:* travel or marriage, or both
*Arrow:* bad news, probably in a letter

*Bells:* marriage
*Birds:* good news
*Bird-cage:* troubles, confinement
*Bird's-nest:* domestic harmony
*Boat:* travel, a visit from a friend, a safe haven
*Book, open:* acquiring knowledge and success
*Book, closed:* be careful of decisions

*Candle:* being helpful; if alight, missionary work
*Castle:* a high position, a legacy
*Cat:* deceit, treachery, quarrels
*Chain, unbroken:* an early marriage or partnership
*Chain, broken:* the breaking of such
*Clouds:* unhappiness, trouble gathering
*Coffin:* bad news, illness, death
*Comet:* a visit from abroad
*Cross:* sacrifice and suffering
*Crown:* good luck, honours, authority

*Dagger:* unexpected danger
*Dog:* a trustworthy friend
*Dragon:* sudden change, unforeseen trouble
*Dot (one):* strengthens whichever sign it be near
*Dots (several):* money

*Eagle:* high success, favourable change of home

*Ear:* news

*Earwig:* gossip

*Egg:* baby, new enterprises

*Elephant:* wisdom, strength, trust

*Envelope:* a letter, news, probably good

*Eye:* be alert and watchful and you will conquer difficulty

*Face:* if pretty or smiling, happiness; if other-wise, the opposite

*Fan:* flirtation

*Fence:* minor set-backs, obstacles

*Fire:* either artistic success, or sudden anger

*Fish:* lucky, peace, plenty, happiness, health and wealth

*Flag:* danger from duties

*Flower:* a wish granted

*Fork:* an important decision to be made

*Fountain:* great success and prosperity

*Gallows:* danger, most likely for your enemies

*Gate:* open, successful progress; closed, a barrier

*Giant:* a strong force in your life

*Giraffe:* trouble, mischief

*Glass:* integrity

*Glove:* you will challenge a decision

*Goat:* obstinacy, onslaught from enemies

*Grapes:* happiness with a Loved One

*Gun:* quarrels, an attack of some kind

*Hammer:* industry, hard work

*Hand:* friendship, understanding; if clenched, an argument

*Harp:* harmony, good fortune, Romance

*Hat:* a gift

*Heart:* close affection, love, marriage

*Helmet:* trust

*Horse:* prosperity, good news

*Horse-shoe:* Good Luck

*Hour-glass:* beware delays, Time is Passing

*House:* domestic peace, security, happiness

*Iceberg:* great danger ahead

*Initials:* someone important to you

*Ink:* a blot, a sullied character

*Insect:* minor irritations and worries

*Ivy-leaf:* faithfulness, a reliable friend

*Jester:* frivolity, or a party

*Jewellery:* a gift or present of value

*Jug:* position of importance, or convivial social occasions

*Kangaroo:* family affection, Domestic Harmony

*Kettle:* illness, probably minor, in the home

*Key:* new interests and opportunities, doors opening

*Kite:* pride may lead to a fall, publicly witnessed

*Knife:* danger, strife, quarrels, broken friendships

*Ladder:* advancement, rising fortunes

*Lamp, lantern:* illumination, wisdom, guidance, monetary success

*Leaf:* receiving good news, prosperity

*Letter:* if clear, good news on its way; if unclear, bad news

*Lines:* if straight, clear progress; if wavy, uncertain progress

*Lion:* strength, greatness, high authority

*Man:* a visitor; with arm outstretched, carrying a gift

*Mask:* beware deception and treachery; guard your own thoughts

*Mermaid:* Temptation

*Moon:* full, romance; waxing, new projects; waning, difficulties

*Mountains:* high aspirations but difficulties to be overcome

*Mushroom:* either sudden growth, or a set-back, in context

*Music notes:* good fortune, enjoyment

*Nail:* maliciousness causing suffering

*Necklace:* complete, a romantic admirer; broken, loss of affections

*Needle:* others will admire and talk about your achievements

*Net:* danger, snares in your path

*Numbers:* interpret in context; may be days or weeks

*Oak:* long life, health, wisdom, strength

*Oar:* safety and help in troubles

*Octopus:* danger, many people are against you

*Old man:* lit. an old man or, a lost opportunity

*Ostrich:* travel over land and sea

*Owl:* a bad omen; gossip and Scandal

*Palm tree:* success, honour, contentment

*Pawn-broker's sign:* lack of material possessions

*Pea-cock:* vanity

*Pear:* comfort, fruitfulness, good fortune

*Pick-axe:* strong determination or, worry connected with work

*Pipe:* calm thought, reflection, consideration

*Priest:* spiritual leadership needed or given

*Question-mark:* be cautious, indecision

*Rabbit:* timidity, be more courageous
*Rainbow:* hope, future happiness
*Rat:* treacherous and malicious enemies
*Raven:* a bad omen, gossip, bad news
*Ring:* friendship, romance, marriage
*Road:* a journey; if straight, no difficulties; if wavy, problems
*Roof:* the home; if unmarried, leaving home; if married, happiness
*Rose:* friendship, happiness, success, popularity

*Scales:* justice or injustice, dependant on the balance
*Scare-crow:* you will be in great material need
*Scissors:* a misunderstanding, a separation
*Scorpion:* vindictiveness, deadly poisonous attack
*Scythe:* cutting off of plans
*See-saw:* your fortunes will rise and fall
*Sheep:* docility, Good Fortune
*Shell:* spreading of good news
*Ship:* travel, prosperity, good fortune
*Shoes:* a change for the better, only if you "step out" strongly
*Snake:* bad luck, enmity, great hate and danger
*Squares:* strength, solidity, sometimes restriction
*Squirrel:* happiness, prosperity, a store of good things
*Star:* health, wealth, Good Luck and happiness
*Sword:* disputes, quarrels

*Saw:* discord, interference from friends

*Table:* a social gathering
*Tent:* travel, an unsettled life

*Thimble:* domestic changes

*Tree:* prosperity and good health

*Tri-angle:* upright, an unexpected legacy; inverted, luck drains away

*Umbrella:* open, caution but protection; closed, assistance denied

*Unicorn:* secret romance, marriage, alliance

*Urn:* chance, lucky money

*Valley:* a dip in fortunes, but they will rise again

*Vase:* your presence gives happiness to others

*Violin:* independence, but beware of egotism

*Volcano:* emotions, passions and instincts may explode harmfully

*Vulture:* loss, theft

*Waterfall:* great good fortune

*Web:* misfortune, entrapment

*Wheel:* achievement, success, advancement

*Wind-mill:* hard work brings business success

*Wings:* messages, good or bad

*Woman:* happiness, pleasure; a Particular Woman

*Yew-tree:* long life

*Yoke:* slavery, domination, a domineering person

*Zebra:* adventure abroad

If a tea leaf symbol is sharp and clear, this strengthens the meaning of the sign, for good or for bad; if it is blurred and vague, uncertainty surrounds the meaning.

If a symbol is INVERTED, then the good meaning may be reversed.

The Reader must draw the symbols together to make a story, as a sign may change its meaning depending on its proximity to others.

The Reader should also be most sensitive to the reactions of the Client; if the Reading appears to be received well, then the Reader may expand on the story with more confidence; but if the Client should show any sign of distress, then the Reader should find something of a Positive Nature to impart from the Leaves, or else draw the Reading to a SWIFT CLOSE.

We should like at this juncture to tell an amusing little tale which occurred, we are told, in the days of the VIRGIN QUEEN ELIZABETH, OF ENGLAND. Tea had but recently come to these shores, and was a great delicacy, enjoyed only in the finest of homes for reason of its scarcity and cost.

The lady of one great house, not wishing to appear *déclassée* in the sight of her peers and acquaintances, acquired two pounds of tea-leaves from a Liverpool merchant. Knowing only that *boiling* was a part of the preparation, she ordered her servant to boil the whole portion of leaves for a good time, perhaps half-an-hour or more. She then threw away the liquid, as one would do with, let us say, cabbage, *spread* the boiled leaves on a biscuit or portion of bread, and ate it. Why, wondered this good lady, was so much fuss made of this new *tea*?

# THE CRYSTAL BALL *or* MIRROR

THE CRYSTAL BALL and magic mirror have surely been used since the beginning of time for seeing far-distant events and those which lie in the future. Although the REV. DR. ARMYTAGE WARE, who is renowned for the orthodoxy of his beliefs, inveighs against their use as "a diabolical and occult practice to be abhorred", we ourselves can see no harm in looking into a *ball* of *glass*; indeed, many find nothing more sinister in the practice than a form of mesmerism or *auto-hypnosis*.

Glass, rather than crystal, it must usually be, as rock-crystal of the necessary clarity and flawlessness is most rare and costly. A professional *Clairvoyant* (literally, one who sees clearly) may use a ball of some six or seven inches in diameter, but there is no reason why one should not obtain good results by using one of three inches, which is more easily to be procured.

Some, indeed, prefer instead of a crystal or glass globe, a polished black mirror, such as was used by the great physician and intelligencer of the Virgin Queen Elizabeth, DR. JOHN DEE, his mirror being a slab of polished cannel-coal.

The *Clairvoyant,* or *Viewer,* or *Scryer* should sit opposite to the Client, with the ball between them, standing on its base upon a table of convenient height, which is covered with a black silk cloth. There must be enough light by which to see, but it must not be too bright, or it might dazzle or distract the *Scryer.*

The atmosphere should be serious, though it need not be solemn. The *Scryer*, concentrating deeply upon the crystal or glass sphere, will see at first CLOUDS forming in its depths. If the Reading be good, the clouds will part to bestow a VISION to the *Scryer*, though the Client see nothing. The *Scryer* should describe what he or she (for both sexes are proficient in this art) sees in the ball, which he might not himself be able to interpret, though his words may make sense to the Client. In this way he is seeing a vision *on behalf of* the Client.

## MAKING ONE'S OWN "CRYSTAL BALL"

**W**e have mentioned Dr. John Dee's black mirror. Any completely clear, or alternatively, polished, black substance may be used for *Scrying*. Some use a pool of black ink; others a glass or bowl of pure distilled water, coloured perhaps with sulphate of iron. The substance of the sphere or mirror, or whatever medium be used, is of no significance in itself; the CRYSTAL BALL (to use the traditional term) is no more than a means by which the *Scryer* may concentrate his vision.

We shall now describe how one may easily make for oneself a most excellent sphere for *Scrying*.

Obtain from an apothecary a strong round-bottomed retort or flask of three to four inches diameter. With a glass-cutter's tool remove most of the neck of the vessel cleanly, so that less than half-an-inch remain. Wash the vessel most thoroughly and carefully, as if it

were the finest crystal wine-glass, in hot soapy water, rinse it well, and leave it to dry completely.

Now fill the vessel completely with the highest quality permanent *black ink*, shaking it gently to ensure that there be no bubbles, and making certain that the ink rise up the full length of the neck. The flask may now be sealed firmly with a cork, ensur-

ing once more that no bubbles of air are trapped within; and the cork should be sealed with pitch or wax so that no air can make its way in at a later time.

A base must also be prepared, either of black stone or of black-stained wood (ebony being ideal); wood is easier, for a hole must be cut to accommodate the neck of the flask, which must be firmly affixed therein.

By making such a Sphere of one's own one can allay the superstitious fears of reactionary minds that the "Crystal Ball" itself has magickal or occult properties. One will also have, at very little cost and no great labour, a sphere which will rival in its efficacy all but the very finest genuine Crystal Balls, and which will by its mere possession enhance one's standing amongst one's peers.

# THE ORACLE
## *of* LOVE

*Magic Squares provide endless fascination for people of all ages. This square is particularly suitable for young people, as it may be consulted to give answers on matters of the Heart, though users should be warned that it may give an answer they would not wish to hear! For this reason, if one of the ladies in your number is known to be seriously in love, or still more if she is to be married, we would suggest that she not be encouraged to use this Oracle.*

The means of use are simple, though one may wrap them around with whatever ritual one desires. The Client, with eyes closed, should hold a question about the one she loves firmly in her mind, but without voicing the question to others present. The Reader, on judging that the Client be ready, should say these words: "Ask the Oracle of Love the question deep in your heart," and the Client should without hesitation point with a quill or other pointed instrument to one of the letters in the Magic Square. The reader may now open her eyes. ■

```
M A L Y B D L A A H O O E E O O L
N A V U F N V O Y P E M O O E N
W P R A R T W G I Y S Y E T I A
L M D N L R L N L A R E O U L D
A R E V N S T H D R A E G T R A
O I M R Y H I P R A S M O I U P
E G F A U M M Y Y E U R R H P W
O T L R L I H E U O F Y O S O D
O Y I Y V P V D N O L O E R E E
E U L U R O R D W R E R W M D L
I P D P I I E I L R W R L S L F
L E I E L E A E G S T S C S Y A
R E H E O A A W I N I N M R N A
E T N T E E D I V L A L T F D T
E O Y O O A O S Y V E V Y L U Y
O E A E O S B O U R R R U E T U
```

THE READER should write that letter on a clean sheet of paper, then count along the same row, the letter *after* the one chosen being "one", the next following being "two", and so on, until the *eighth* letter be reached, and this should be written down after the letter first selected. When the right-hand edge be reached, the counting should continue without interruption from the first letter on the left-hand side of the following line. The process should continue with great care for accuracy until the Reader has worked through the whole Magic Square, continuing from the bottom line to the top, finally reaching the letter eight before the one first chosen, and writing down the eighth letter each time, with one Important Caveat: the first letter lighted upon in the top row should be underlined when it be written upon the paper.

Let us assume that the young lady Client has the question in her heart: "Should I give my heart to the tall, dashing officer who has been paying me court?" The letter she first indicates is the sixth from the left in the twelfth row, "E". The eighth letter following this is "S", followed by "A", "R", and so on. Proceeding around the square the Reader will write down the following, underlining the first character reached in the top row:

E S A R E F A L S E <u>D</u> O N O T T R U S T H I M H I S P R O M I S

The answer should then be read, commencing from the underlined letter.

The oracle of love has given a clear warning to the young lady which she would do well to heed! It is as well to conduct these consultations with the Oracle privately to save the *blushes* of the Client when all hear the answer it gives; and certainly none of the gentlemen should be present for the Reading.

Like all Oracles and other means of Prediction and Divination, this Magic Square or Oracle of Love should be approached with respect, for it can be capricious if treated carelessly. It should not be consulted more than thrice in one evening, and then only for three different Clients; and on no account should any Client return to the Oracle within a seven-day, with the same question or any other.

The answers of the oracle of love are startling in their accuracy, and many are amazed that it should be able to speak to them so clearly, believing that it must have Occult powers. Some young people with mathematical inclinations (and in these enlightened days of *our queen's* Empire there are some such even amongst the educated ladies of our acquaintance) ☞

will understand the principles upon which the Magic Square operates, though none can say why it should give one answer rather than another.

For most young people the ORACLE OF LOVE will provide hours of amusement, though some may find its answers disturbing. When I first showed this Oracle to my friend the Rev. Dr. Armytage Ware, who I should remind you can no longer be described as young, if indeed he ever could have been, he was deeply shocked at its response to his question (which he had not, of course, revealed to me), and could not be persuaded that it was not calling upon Occult powers, even when in desperation I explained to him the logical workings of the Magic Square. I shall not, of course, out of delicacy reveal the answer that was given to him.

# KAR-MI

**PRINCE KAR-MI**

PRESENTING

**MYSTERIES OF THE SPIRIT WORLD**

AND DEMONSTRATIONS OF

**OCCULT POWERS**

**ASTOUNDING FEATS**

# THE CAREER ORACLE

*This Magic Square will give advice to the young man who is troubled about his future, and wishes guidance for the years ahead of him. In operation it is much the same as the Oracle of Love, with this exception: that it be the FIFTH letter which must in each case be written down.*

```
H T F N F A A O O E
R K R T A D E E W R
W N I E N O O G A O
R T N L T K A S T F
B D H H O R V O Y R
I I R B Y N C E U O
G E S T U S B C C R
R L A O F E I L N U
W N L T T A D Y E U
R L O N R D Y U T E
```

*Suppose that the young man ask the Career Oracle this question: "Should I follow my father into the City or should I join the Diplomatic Service?" With his eyes closed he selects the third letter in the seventh row, an "S". The* FIFTH *letter to follow this is a "C", then an "A" and an "L". Marking the first letter to be encountered in the top row as before, he receives this answer:*

S C A L L Y O U <u>F</u> O R E I G N S H O R E

*The Career Oracle, it would seem, has peered into his heart.*

*It is wise to restrict the consultation of this Oracle to ONCE per Client as, being of a smaller size, its range of answers is necessarily more limited.*

*For those who are able to deduce the means by which these Oracles work, it is a pleasant enough occupation on an afternoon when it is raining to devise MAGIC SQUARES of one's own to provide answers on any subject of one's choice. If after several months the young ladies become familiar with the answers of the ORACLE OF LOVE, one could, with great care and without telling one's young friends, design a new ORACLE OF LOVE with different answers, making sure that some promise their heart's desire whilst others warn them to tread with care the Path of Love.*

# WHO SHALL I MARRY?
# WHEN SHALL I MARRY?

THESE ARE questions which every young lady seems to have at the forefront of her thoughts, almost from the moment she can formulate those thoughts into words, right up to the moment when she does, indeed, marry.

The questions of *WHO*, and *WHEN*, are, it seems, every girl's highest preoccupation, and many are the means by which they seek to find the answers. Here we shall mention just a few of them, as are found in every part of these islands. These are suitable for younger girls, aged maybe nine to four-teen.

## TO FIND *his* NAME

The young lady should peel an apple carefully, using a sharp knife, in such a way that the peel is all in one long continuous strip. She should then throw this over her left shoulder, and if it lands on the floor in one piece, it will show the initial of the one she will love.

If a girl should find a piece of cotton on her dress, she should wind it around the ring finger of her left hand, counting how many times it encircles it. If only once, then the man she will marry will have the initial **A**; if twice, **B**, if three times, **C**, and so on.

One can always hope to dream of the man one is to marry, and many are the ways by which this may be achieved. The one we prefer is performed upon SAINT AGNES' EVE, and (in the words of the *Rev. Dr. Armytage Ware,* who is most insistant that this be said) is thus morally instructive, for the blessed Saint, three-hundred years after the birth of our Saviour, preferred to die than be forced to marry against her will.

Upon the TWENTIETH DAY OF JANUARY, which is the *Eve of Saint Agnes' Day*, the young lady should bake a cake of flour, eggs, water and salt, maintaining her silence the while. She should then mark her initials on the cake, and recite these words in an attitude of PIETY:

> *Sweet Saint Agnes, work thy fast*
> *If ever I be to marry man*
> *Or ever man to marry me*
> *I hope him this night to see*

She should set the cake by the fire that it might bake slowly through the night, and retire to her chamber to sleep, and to dream of the man she will marry. Some say that on the morrow she should examine the cake most carefully, for beside her own initials might be found those of her **FUTURE LOVER**. ☛

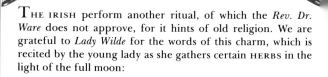

THE IRISH perform another ritual, of which the *Rev. Dr. Ware* does not approve, for it hints of old religion. We are grateful to *Lady Wilde* for the words of this charm, which is recited by the young lady as she gathers certain HERBS in the light of the full moon:

> *Moon, Moon, tell unto me*
> *When my true love I shall see.*
> *What fine clothes am I to wear?*
> *How many children shall I bear?*
> *For if my love comes not to me*
> *Dark and dismal my life will be.*

From the place where she finds the herbs, the young lady must cut three pieces of soil with a black-hafted knife, and upon taking them home, tie them into her LEFT STOCKING with her RIGHT GARTER, placing the whole beneath her pillow; whereupon she will dream of her **TRUE LOVE**.

"There is superstition in avoiding superstition."
FRANCES BACON

## TO CONFIRM *his* AFFECTIONS

The young lady and her intended should each place a nut by the fire, so that they are side by side. (The maiden may spare her lover's blushes, or perform this in his absence, by placing both nuts herself, so long as she call one by his name, and the other by her own.) If the nuts burn steadfastly together, then the couple shall indeed be married; but if one burn alone, or if one or both the nuts *CRACK VIOLENTLY* so that the nuts are separated, then so shall the couple be.

If she write down her own name, and that of the one she loves, and crosses out the letters they share in common, those that remain may give an indication of the continuing of their affection, in the following wise: with each name separately, the girl should call out the words "Love, Marry, Hate, Adore", with one word to each singular letter. The last word named will predict the future for that person. Thus:

/ / L / M  / H A L M H / : Hate     L M H / /   / / A L M / H : Hate
E T H E L   B U R R O W S          J A M E S   B E C K E T T

Ethel and James are clearly not destined for each other!

# TO FIND
# OUT WHEN

From earliest days flowers have been tokens of love; did not the one beloved of Solomon in his Song name herself "the Rose of Sharon and the Lily of the Valleys"? So to-day our young ladies turn to flowers to find when they will be joined with their beloved.

There are two main ways by which this may be done. The first is to pick a FRESH DAISY and pluck the petals one by one, while reciting the words: *"This year, Next year, Some-time, Never"*. The last petal will tell the maiden's marriage fate. Alternatively she might pick a DANDELION CLOCK, hold it before her lips, and blow briskly and shortly. The number of times she needs to blow before all the seeds are scattered will be the number of years until she wed.

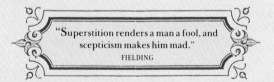

"Superstition renders a man a fool, and scepticism makes him mad."
FIELDING

In early Spring the young lady who hears for the first time that year a *CUCKOO CALL*, should speak to the cuckoo thus:

> *Cuckoo, Cuckoo, answer me true*
> *This question which I ask of you*
> *I beg that truly you tell to me*
> *In how many years I will married be*

When the cuckoo replies she should count the number of his calls, for this will be the number of years until she is wed.

# ZODIACAL BIRTH SIGNS

Zodiacal Birth Signs, which are determined by when in the year one's birthday falls, can tell the practiced enquirer much about one's character, even without performing the long and very complicated business of drawing an individual star chart, or HOROSCOPE, which by showing the position of each planet against the constellations of stars behind it at the very moment of one's birth, describes the beneficent or malefic influences of these ASTRONOMICAL CONJUNCTIONS on one's life.

Each of us has a Zodiacal Birth Sign, determined simply by our date of birth as in the following table; and each of us will show some of the characteristics ascribed to our own sign — though those with expertise in this complex subject say that there are many other factors which also affect our character. ☞

March 21st – April 19th
*ARIES, the Ram*
Strong, determined, energetic, but can be
domineering.

April 20th – May 20th
*TAURUS, the Bull*
Patient, tenacious, reliable, but can be
possessive.

May 21st – June 21st
*GEMINI, the Twins*
Intelligent, inventive, versatile, but can be
mercurial.

June 22nd – July 22nd
*CANCER, the Crab*
Home-loving, romantic, considerate, but
can be over-sensitive.

July 23rd – August 22nd
*LEO, the Lion*
Independent, courageous, loyal, but can
be too proud.

August 23rd – September 22nd
*VIRGO, the Virgin*
Sensible, practical, dependable, but can
be over-fussy.

September 23rd – October 23rd
*LIBRA, the Scales*
Well-balanced, tolerant, diplomatic, but
can be easily influenced.

October 24th – November 21st
*SCORPIO, the Scorpion*
Powerful, passionate, compelling, but can
be uncompromising.

November 22nd – December 21st
*SAGITTARIUS, the Archer*
Mature, open, enthusiastic, but can be
impulsively angry.

December 22nd – January 19th
*CAPRICORN, the Goat*
Good leader, ambitious, hard-working,
but can be capricious.

January 20th – February 18th
*AQUARIUS, the Water-Carrier*
Charming, independent, non-conformist,
but can be wilful.

February 19th – March 20th
*PISCES, the Fishes*
Friendly, gentle, helpful, but can be easily
distracted.

## CHARACTERS *and* BIRTH-DATES

Even this small amount of information can be used at a dinner party, in several amusing ways. One could simply ask one's guests for their BIRTH-DATE, and then tell them the type of character they are supposed to have; this can lead to long and interesting *Discussion*.

Alternatively, and for greater amusement, one can write out on a large sheet of card all of the *"CHARACTER ATTRIBUTES"* as listed above, with neither the dates nor the names of the Zodiacal signs attached. You then ask all your guests to choose which they think is closest to how they really are, and which is closest to their husband or wife, and to write these down against their names on sheets of paper which you distribute to them.

You then take all the sheets of paper and write down against each name the *ZODIACAL SIGN* relating to those characteristics, with the dates given in the list. 🐖

Finally, you ask each person for his or her DATE OF BIRTH, and write this by their name, using a different coloured pencil so that none may accuse you of cheating.

The results will be quite fascinating. If these characteristics were quite randomly assigned, each person would have one chance in twelve of choosing the attributes linked with their own, or their spouse's birth-date. You will be amazed at how many have chosen the correct attributes, and they will be amazed at your knowing the time of year that each was born.

If all your guests know each other well, they can each write down the characteristics of all the others. When you work out the results, you will find that some people have been correctly identified by practically everyone present; whilst others, whose characters are perhaps more complex, have not been so readily and accurately identified.

It may be of interest that this whole matter of *ZODIACAL SIGNS* was recently preached against at length by the *Rev. Dr. Armytage Ware*. Regrettably I am unable to pass on any of his no doubt strongly argued and cogent points as I unfortunately fell asleep shortly after the beginning of his sermon.

THE MYSTICAL WHEEL OF PYTHAGORAS

THE FIRST FIVE COLOURED DESIGNS BY RAPHAEL & R. CRUIKSHANK.

# THE SAME
# BIRTH-DATE

*I*f you are hosting quite a large Dinner Party, with more than twelve guests, you can astound them all in this way: simply look around the drawing room and announce in a quiet but confident manner that you believe that two of the people in the room share the same *BIRTH-DAY*.

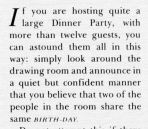

Do not attempt this if there are fewer than TWELVE persons in the room. Clearly the more people are present, the more likely you are of being proved correct, but the remarkable fact is (and this has been proven mathematically) that if there are twelve persons present in a room, **there is a greater than even chance** that two of them will share the same BIRTH-DATE.

If on any occasion you are proved wrong, as is bound to happen from time to time by the immutable *Laws of Chance*, you will be more likely to gain the sympathy of your guests than their derision, for it may almost be guaranteed that two people will have BIRTH-DAYS only one day apart.

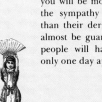

# LUCKY DAYS *of the* MONTH

## FORTUNATE DAYS

In *January,* six days: the 1st, 2nd, 15th, 26th, 27th, and 28th.

In *February,* four days: the 11th, 21st, 25th, and 26th.

In *March,* two days: the 10th, and 24th.

In *April,* five days: the 6th, 15th, 16th, 20th, and 28th.

In *May,* three days: the 3rd, 18th, and 31st.

In *June,* five days: the 10th, 11th, 15th, 22nd, and 25th.

In *July,* three days: the 9th, 15th, and 28th.

In *August,* six days: the 6th, 7th, 10th, 11th, 19th, and 25th.

In *September,* five days: the 4th, 8th, 17th, 18th, and 23rd.

In *October,* five days: the 3rd, 7th, 16th, 21st and 22nd.

In *November,* three days: the 5th, 14th, and 20th.

In *December,* six days: the 15th, 19th, 20th, 22nd, 23rd, and 25th.

# UNFORTUNATE DAYS

In *January*, seven days: the 3rd, 4th, 6th, 13th, 14th, 20th, and 21st.

In *February*, seven days: the 3rd, 7th, 9th, 12th, 16th, 17th, and 23rd.

In *March*, eight days: the 1stm 2nd, 5th, 8th, 12th, 16th, 28th, and 29th.

In *April*, two days: the 24th, and 25th.

In *May*, five days: the 17th, 20th, 27th, 29th, and 30th.

In *June*, eight days: the 1stm 5th, 6th, 9th, 12th, 16th, 18th, and 24th.

In *July*, four days: the 3rd, 10th, 17th, and 18th.

In *August*, two days: the 15th, and 20th.

In *September*, two days: the 9th, and 16th.

In *October*, six days: the 4th, 9th, 11th, 17th, 27th, and 31st.

In *November*, four days: the 3rd, 9th, 10th, and 21st.

In *December*, two days: the 14th, and 21st.

## **LUCKY DAYS of the WEEK**

If a person have his measure taken for new clothes on a *Sunday*, he will be sorrowful and crying. If on a *Monday*, he will have ample food and provisions. If on a *Tuesday*, his clothes will be burnt. If on a *Wednesday*, he will enjoy happiness and tranquillity. If on a *Thursday*, he will be good and propitious. If on a *Friday*, he will get into prison. If on a *Saturday*, he will experience numerous troubles and misfortunes.

If one put on a new suit of clothes on a *Sunday*, he will experience happiness and ease. If on a *Monday*, his clothes will tear. If on a *Tuesday*, even if he stand in water, his clothes will catch fire. If on a *Wednesday*, he will readily obtain a new suit. If on a *Thursday*, his dress will appear neat and elegant. If on a *Friday*, as long as the suit remains new, he will be happy and delighted. If on a *Saturday*, he will be taken ill.

If a person put on a new suit of clothes in the *morning*, he will become wealthy and fortunate. If at *noon*, he will appear elegant. If at about *sunset*, he will become wretched. If in the *evening*, he will continue ill.

If a person bathe on *Sunday*, he will experience affliction. If on *Monday*, his property will increase. If on *Tuesday*, he will labour under anxiety of mind. If on *Wednesday*, he will increase in beauty. If on *Thursday*, his property will increase. If on *Friday*, all his sins will be forgiven. If on *Saturday*, all his ailments will be removed.

# THE ORACLE of DESTINY

THIS TABLE is to be tried on any day of the week, *Wednesdays excepted*, which is held by the Greek sages and the professors of the noble science of Astrology, as unlucky for such pursuits, casting nativities, or interpreting dreams. How far they may be right, the translator does not pretend to judge: it is certain they maintain that opinion. Also, that no person should search into the knowledge of future events on their *natal* day.

First prick in the middle of the table, with your eyelids closed, to find the planet that is to fall to your share, and, having found it out, do the same in the circle belonging to it for the given number.

## AQUARIUS

*1* A happy lot, especially in marriage.

*2* Several lovers, and select the worst.

*3* An unexpected event that will enrich you.

*4* You will benefit more by the dead than by the living.

*5* You will be enriched through the means of a foreigner whom you have not yet seen.

*6* The best of blessing – health and happiness.

## PISCES

*1* A good conscience will be your chief treasure in old age, after many changes.

*2* Great benefit from good children – you will survive most of them.

*3* Voyages to sea, and settlement abroad.

*4* A great loss through a false friend or lover.

*5* You will better yourself in marriage.

*6* If you a widowhood should gain,
Long you will not it retain,
You're born to a third marriage chain.

## ARIES

*1* If you do not get rich by your twenty-ninth year, you never will, for that is your utmost elevation.

*2* A speedy prosperity when you think Fate has deserted you, by most unlooked for but honest means – so do not despair.

*3* Face danger boldly. You are born to surmount difficulties, and have a happy meridian and end.

*4* You will gain experience rather too dear, but prosper after your lesson.

*5* Jealousy will be the marplot of your peace.

*6* You will not wed your first love, but the loss is all for the best.

## TAURUS

*1* You will have riches, but an ill-tempered mate.

*2* Within a month you will find something of consequence.

*3* Several children, but not to your bliss.

*4* A debt contracted by imprudence that will annoy you.

*5* Important news on the road from afar.

*6* A strange home within a year.

## GEMINI

*1* A new lover, but a constant and valuable one.
*2* Perfidy is about to wound you.
*3* There's a person has made a promise which you depend on, and they intend to keep it, but will not be able, so prepare your mind.
*4* Many flowers in your path.
*5* Deceit from an unexpected quarter.
*6* A foreign letter of interest.

## CANCER

*1* Great promotion at hand.
*2* An enviable fate is to come.
*3* A speedy change in present affairs.
*4* A failure in trade to your detriment.
*5* A sincere friend of the other sex.
*6* A party of pleasure, from which great events will arise.

## LEO

*1* A moonlight walk will be long remembered.
*2* Many changes at hand.
*3* A quarrel with your lover.
*4* You have a secret rival.
*5* You have a false confidant.
*6* The next favour you ask will be granted.

# VIRGO

*1* Gives you prosperity, and the chance of a number in Capricorn.

*2* Gives you good children, and mark three in Capricorn.

*3* Two husbands, and to try for a number in Capricorn.

*4* A speedy offer you had best reject.

*5* The loss of what you can never regain.

*6* Speedy reconciliation, when you desire it.

# LIBRA

*1* You will gain many useful friends.

*2* Refers you to Capricorn to try a number.

*3* You will suffer by scandal.

*4* You will go abroad within three years.

*5* You will suffer by carelessness.

*6* You will lose by a wager.

# VENUS

*1* Early marriage and happiness.

*2* Too many lovers, and some tears.

*3* Crossings in love and amorous perplexities.

*4* An intrigue stopped in good time.

*5* A false lover and a perfidious friend.

*6* Advancement through marriage.

## SCORPIO

1 A bustling life, but no advancement.
2 A better end than beginning.
3 Success by trade or servitude.
4 A sudden and happy elevation.
5 A new offer and establishment.
6 Sagittarius, No. 3, will give the answer.

## SAGITTARIUS

1 Your planets give a happy issue to your own endeavours –
depend not on others for support.
2 An easy life, with few cares to depress you.
3 Your planets give strife and discord.
4 Your partner will be too fond of the bottle and glass.
5 You will soon form a lasting friendship.
6 You will soon gain what you at present most desire.

## CAPRICORN

1 The best of blessings – health and happiness.
2 An excellent offer will soon be made to your advantage.
3 Unexpected prosperity from persons at present unknown.
4 Fate has good things in store for you.
5 You will sow with toil, but reap a golden harvest.
6 You will soon have cause to rejoice at an event that is going on
with your present knowledge.

FINIS